JAMIE DORNAN BIOGRAPHY

Unveiling The Hidden Truth Behind The Cause Of Illness, Health Status, Career Journey, Wife, Kids, And Net Worth Of a famous Actor Of Fifty Shades Of Grey movie

Josefina D. Comfort

Copyright page

Copyright © josefina D.Comfort, 2024

All rights reserved. No part of this publication may be reproduced, distributed, or transmitted in any form or by any means, including photocopying, recording, or other electronic or mechanical methods, without the prior written permission of the publisher, except in the case of brief quotations embodied in critical reviews and certain other noncommercial uses permitted by copyright law.

TABLE OF CONTENTS

Copyright page.. 1
TABLE OF CONTENTS... 2
INTRODUCTION.. 4
CHAPTER ONE.. 9
   Who is Jamie Dornan?... 9
   Roots and Beginnings: A Belfast Childhood........... 11
CHAPTER TWO... 15
   Stepping into the Spotlight: Modeling and Early Music Career... 15
   Breaking Through Acquiring Positions and Creating Energy.. 17
   The Tipping Point: Global Recognition and Fifty Shades of Grey...21
CHAPTER FOUR...25
   Acting Challenges and Diverse Roles Beyond Christian Grey..25
CHAPTER FIVE... 28
   Love, Family, and Personal Life: Balancing Stardom with Privacy...28
   Jamie Dornan's Wife...30
   Jamie Dornan Kids... 33
   Welcoming the Firstborns: Dulcie and Elva............. 33
   Jamie Dornan and Dulcie... 34
   Philanthropy and Advocacy: Using Influence for Good..37

JAMIE DORNAN BIOGRAPHY

CHAPTER SEVEN **41**
   Facing Scrutiny and Overcoming Obstacles:
   Maintaining Integrity 41

CHAPTER EIGHT **45**
   Post-Fifty Shades: Reclaiming his narrative and
   artistic freedom 45

CHAPTER NINE **52**
   Producing and Directing: Expanding his creative
   footprint 52
   A Tapestry of Artistic Evolution: 55
   Music: A Sanctuary of the Soul: 58
   Jamie Dornan was rushed to the hospital with
   symptoms of a heart attack after coming into contact
   with toxic caterpillars 62
   Treatment and Recovery: 65
   Dornan movies and TV shows 66
   Early Beginnings: Stepping into the Spotlight
   (2006-2011) 66
   Jamie Dornan's Salary and Net Worth 71
   Jamie Dornan's Fifty Shades Salary: From a Modest
   Sum to Millions 73
   Jamie Dornan on The Late Late Show: A Dashing
   Blend of Charm, Heartfelt Moments, and Irish Craic .. 77

CONCLUSION **81**

INTRODUCTION

Forget the brooding billionaire, the chiseled heartthrob, the neatly packaged persona plastered across magazine covers. Jamie Dornan, the name that evokes intrigue and fascination, is far more than a single shade painted on the Hollywood canvas. He is an enigma, a tapestry woven with threads of artistic ambition, unwavering family devotion, and a genuine desire to contribute to the world beyond the spotlight. Born in the quaint town of Hollywood, Northern Ireland, Dornan's roots run deep in the fertile soil of storytelling. An artistic spirit bloomed early, leading him to explore music and drama throughout his school years. A brief detour into the world of modeling catapulted him into the public eye, his chiseled features earning him the moniker "The Golden Torso." Yet, beneath the captivating facade, a yearning for deeper expression flickered within.

Modeling provided a platform, a springboard for his true passion: acting. His film debut in Sofia Coppola's "Marie Antoinette" marked a turning point, followed by critically acclaimed performances in "Once Upon a Time" and the chilling "The Fall." Then came the role that thrust him into the global spotlight: Christian Grey in the "Fifty Shades" trilogy. But Dornan refused to be defined by a single shade. He actively sought roles that showcased his versatility, defying typecasting and expectations. In the poignant "Belfast," he delivered a nuanced performance that resonated with audiences and critics alike, showcasing his emotional depth and range. His comedic timing shined brightly in the quirky "Barb and Star Go to Vista Del Mar," proving his adaptability and willingness to embrace diverse genres. Upcoming projects like the spy thriller "Heart of Stone" and the dark drama "A Haunting in Venice" further solidify his commitment to artistic exploration, refusing to be confined by any single box.

In 2023, while vacationing in Portugal with friends, Dornan encountered a potentially dangerous situation. Contact with processionary moth caterpillars resulted in an unexpected medical emergency that landed him in the hospital. Thankfully, after receiving prompt medical attention, Dornan made a full recovery. This incident, though unsettling, served as a reminder of the unpredictable nature of life and the importance of awareness and responsible interaction with the natural world. Beyond the captivating performances and the sculpted features lies a man with a heart attuned to the rhythm of love and responsibility. Married to musician Amelia Warner, Dornan cherishes his role as a father to their three daughters. He fiercely protects their privacy, striving to provide them with a normal upbringing despite the glare of the spotlight. Fatherhood has significantly impacted his life and career choices, prioritizing roles that allow him to spend quality time with his family.

But Dornan's compassion extends far beyond his immediate circle. He actively supports various charitable causes, focusing on children's health and environmental issues. His participation in fundraising events and lending his voice to campaigns demonstrate his commitment to making a positive difference in the world. He understands the platform his success has provided and uses it to shine a light on issues close to his heart. Dornan is refreshingly down-to-earth, possessing a self-deprecating humor that disarms and endears him to audiences. He openly discusses his struggles with fame and the challenges of balancing his career with family life. This genuineness resonates with viewers, revealing a relatable human being beneath the celebrity facade. He doesn't shy away from poking fun at himself, showcasing a vulnerability that endears him further.

This book is an invitation to embark on a captivating journey, a deep dive into the life and soul of Jamie Dornan. We'll delve deeper into his acting process, exploring the intricacies of his craft and the challenges he has faced. We'll analyze the impact of the "Fifty Shades" phenomenon, separating fact from fiction and examining its influence on his career and public perception. We'll also shed light on his musical influences, philanthropic endeavors, and the values that guide his personal and professional life.

Prepare to be surprised, intrigued, and ultimately, inspired by the man who is Jamie Dornan. He is more than just an actor; he is a talented artist, a devoted family man, and a kind soul who uses his platform to make a positive impact. Join us as we unveil the man behind the mystery, revealing the layers that make him who he truly is. Turn the page and begin your journey into the captivating world of Jamie Dornan, a man who proves that beneath the shades lies a tapestry woven with artistry, heart, and genuine humanity.

CHAPTER ONE

Who is Jamie Dornan?

Jamie Dornan, the name instantly conjures images of brooding billionaires, charismatic heartthrobs, and captivating performances. But beyond the silver screen allure and the media headlines lies a complex and multifaceted individual whose journey deserves a closer look. This exploration delves into the life and career of Dornan, peeling back the layers of the public persona to reveal the artist, the family man, and the human being beneath.

From Northern Ireland to the World Stage:

Born in Hollywood, County Down, in 1982, Dornan's roots are firmly planted in Northern Ireland. Raised in a supportive family, his artistic inclinations emerged early, leading him to explore music and drama during his school years. After a brief stint at Middlesex University, London, he embarked on a successful modeling career, gracing the covers of renowned magazines and becoming known for his chiseled physique, earning him the nickname "The Golden Torso."

The Actor: From Model to Leading Man:

While modeling provided a platform, Dornan's true passion lay in acting. His film debut in Sofia Coppola's "Marie Antoinette" (2006) marked a turning point. He subsequently garnered critical acclaim for his portrayal of Sheriff Graham Humbert in the ABC series "Once Upon a Time" (2011-2013). Then came the role that catapulted him to global stardom: Christian Grey in the "Fifty Shades" trilogy (2015-2018). Despite mixed reviews for the films, Dornan's captivating performance solidified his place as a leading man.

Beyond the Shades: Exploring Artistic Diversity:

Dornan has consciously sought roles that showcase his versatility and defy typecasting. He delivered a nuanced performance in Kenneth Branagh's semi-autobiographical film "Belfast" (2021), earning numerous accolades and demonstrating his emotional range. His comedic timing shone in "Barb and Star Go to Vista Del Mar" (2021), proving his adeptness at lighthearted fare. His upcoming projects, including the spy thriller "Heart of Stone" and the drama series "A Haunting in Venice," further demonstrate his commitment to diverse and challenging roles.

The Musician: A Creative Pursuit:

Music remains a constant in Dornan's life. He co-founded the folk band Sons of Jim in his early twenties, demonstrating his songwriting and musical talents. While acting took precedence, he continues to contribute music to films like "Belfast" and occasionally performs live. This artistic outlet allows him to connect with his roots and express himself in a different creative form.

Roots and Beginnings: A Belfast Childhood

Jamie Dornan was not always meant for the big screen, despite his name being associated with sultry charm and Hollywood glamor. His journey starts in Belfast,

Northern Ireland, a bustling working-class city, rather than in the flash and glamor of Los Angeles. Jamie was born on May 1, 1982, in the coastal town of Hollywood, County Down. Jim, an obstetrician, and Lorna, a nurse, were the parents of three children. Jamie was the youngest. His early years were braided together by the strands of religion, family, and the constant background of the "Troubles," the protracted war that tore Northern Ireland apart for decades. Despite not being actively engaged in the fighting, the Dornans were still affected by it because of constant tension in the air, security checks, and bomb scares. Nonetheless, Jamie had a happy and comfortable upbringing within their house. He was a lively and naughty toddler who was sometimes called "full of beans." His two elder sisters, Liesa and Jessica, were his favorite people to be around, and he also enjoyed the company of his extended family, who got together often for raucous feasts and intense discussions. An important part of Jamie's upbringing was his faith. His parents were frequent churchgoers, and both sets of grandparents were Methodist lay preachers. This gave him a strong sense of morality and a firm conviction in empathy and compassion, qualities that he would later demonstrate in his acting career.

Jamie's passion for athletics counterbalanced his academic endeavors. Playing for the Belfast Harlequins, he was a standout rugby player who envisioned a career on the field. But acting started to ignite another passion of his. He took part in school productions, including parts in the Christmas pantomime and musicals like "Bugsy Malone". His depiction as Widow Twankey won him his first drama award, demonstrating his innate charm and stage presence.

When Jamie's mother Lorna passed away from pancreatic cancer while he was only 16 years old, tragedy hit. He was not changed by this tragic loss, which also gave him a resilient mindset that would help him overcome obstacles in the future. Another setback occurred a year later when four of his close friends perished unexpectedly in a vehicle accident. Even though they were very painful, these losses made Jamie face his own death and gave him a greater determination to live life to the fullest. He turned his sorrow into artistic endeavors, turning to literature and music for comfort. His deep voice and musical aptitude were shown when he temporarily joined pals in a folk band.

CHAPTER TWO

Stepping into the Spotlight: Modeling and Early Music Career

Following his graduation from Methodist College Belfast, Jamie Dornan found himself unsure about his next move. After a short enrollment at Teesside University, he left because London's charms and the possibility of something more drew him in. His family pushed him to consider modeling because of his unquestionable good looks and innate charm. He was reluctant at first, but in 2001 he gave in and was thrown into the cutthroat world of fashion.

There were ups and downs in his initial modeling endeavor. Despite being a participant, he was ousted before the finals of the reality program "Model Behaviour". Unfazed, he joined Select Model Management and soon started getting commercials for big names like Hugo Boss, Abercrombie & Fitch, and Aquascutum. He shot to worldwide stardom in 2004 when he signed on as the face of Calvin Klein, starring opposite Eva Mendes in a seductive ad. He became known as "The Golden Torso," cemented his place as a rising star in the modeling industry with his toned body and menacing glare.

Even with his fame as a model, Jamie's true passion was music. His love of creating songs and performing had always been there, and in 2006 he and his friend David Alexander founded the folk band Sons of Jim. The Scottish singer-songwriter KT Tunstall toured with the band, and they released two songs, "Fairytale" and "My Burning Sun." The band had some success. Their sound, which combined reflective words with soulful vocals, demonstrated Jamie's narrative skills and creative sensibility.

However, managing the duties of a band with a budding modeling career proved difficult. Sons of Jim broke apart in 2008, which put Jamie in a difficult situation. He kept modeling, appearing on the covers of high-end publications like GQ and Vogue, but he also longed for a more satisfying creative outlet. The attraction of acting, which had always appealed to him, started to entice him more. He was cast as Count Axel Fersen in Sofia Coppola's historical drama "Marie Antoinette" in 2006. This was his first screen appearance. Even though it was a small role, it gave him a taste of the entertainment industry and stoked his interest in performing. He started taking acting lessons to hone his craft and be ready for the next phase of his career.

Breaking Through Acquiring Positions and Creating Energy

Jamie Dornan started his acting career with a fire for success and an unyielding determination. His formative years were characterized by a string of modest parts in TV shows and movies, each of which served as a springboard for greater things. He starred in the BBC Three drama "Nice to Meet You" and the independent feature "Shadows in the Sun" in 2009. Even though these parts didn't attract a lot of notice, they gave him invaluable experience and helped him hone his skills.

The year 2011 was a sea change for him when he was cast as Sheriff Graham Humberly on the ABC fantasy series "Once Upon a Time." Despite being a recurrent character, the job gave him more exposure to the public and increased his notoriety. His portrayal of the endearing and valiant sheriff struck a chord with viewers because of his subtle sensitivity.

He was able to get a major part in the 2012 British television movie "Death and Nightingales," which was adapted from the Eugene McCabe book. His depiction of Liam Ward, a troubled and complicated young man enmeshed in violence, won praise from critics for its emotional depth and unadulterated passion. His dramatic range was on display in this performance, which made him an impressive performer. But the part that would catapult Jamie Dornan into the public eye was still to come. 2013 saw him cast as Paul Spector, a serial murderer, in the highly regarded BBC psychological thriller "The Fall." Jamie, who was paired with Gillian Anderson, gave a terrifying performance that perfectly encapsulated the depth and severity of his role. He won the Irish Film and Television Award for Best Actor in a Lead Role in Drama as well as accolades from all around the world for his enthralling performance, which struck a balance between charm and threat.

"The Fall" turned into a worldwide sensation, securing Jamie's status as a rising star and enthralling viewers everywhere. He took advantage of his newfound success by selecting a variety of occupations that best suited his skills. He played Jan Kubiš, a Czechoslovakian soldier engaged in the killing of Nazi leader Reinhard Heydrich, in the historical drama "Anthropoid" that aired in 2014. He portrayed Will Scarlet in the live-action "Robin Hood" adaption the next year.

Jamie skillfully walked the tightrope between indie and mainstream endeavors throughout this time, accumulating a solid and diverse body of work. He persisted in looking for demanding parts that let him push the limits of his creativity. Acting as Commandant Pat Quinlan in the military film "The Siege of Jadotville"

(2016), he demonstrated his leadership and fortitude under duress.

CHAPTER THREE

The Tipping Point: Global Recognition and Fifty Shades of Grey

The entertainment world was rocked in 2013 when a casting call for the film version of E.L. James' erotic book "Fifty Shades of Grey" was released. The novel had become an international sensation due to its BDSM ideas and sexual material, but there were special difficulties when adapting it for the big screen. It was difficult to find performers who were willing to play the complicated and contentious characters of college student Anastasia Steele and wealthy Christian Grey.

Still riding high after "The Fall," Jamie Dornan was hesitant to go into the audition at first. He was initially concerned about the story's sexual content and the possibility of negative publicity, but in the end, he was drawn to the creative challenge and the chance to play a character with depth. He studied BDSM procedures and studied Christian psychology to learn about his needs and motives to prepare himself for the part. The rumor that Jamie Dornan has been selected to play Christian Grey leaked in October 2013. Filming for the role of Anastasia Steele, played by Dakota Johnson, started early in 2014. The creation was cloaked in mystery, which heightened interest in conjecture.

After breaking box office records with its February 2015 release, the movie went on to earn over $571 million worldwide. The movie "Fifty Shades of Grey" became a cultural sensation, evoking strong emotions and provoking intense discussions over how it portrayed consent, romance, and power relationships. Critics gave the movie mixed reviews, however, they praised Jamie Dornan's performance for being vulnerable and intense. He successfully conveyed the mysterious spirit of Christian Grey by striking a balance between his tyrannical manner and his delicate and yearning moments. The role instantly made him a household figure and propelled him to international acclaim.

But the increased celebrity also brought with it its own set of difficulties. Jamie had to deal with the public's opinion of him and his affiliation with the contentious figure, which drew harsh criticism from both supporters and detractors. He managed the attention with poise and skill, avoiding tabloid controversy while displaying his humor and intellect in interviews.

Despite the flurry that surrounded "Fifty Shades of Grey," Jamie didn't waver from his artistic vision. In the follow-up films, "Fifty Shades Darker" (2017) and "Fifty Shades Freed" (2018), he played the same character and continued to delve into the subtleties of Christian and Anastasia's relationship. Even though the film's box office performance fell short of the original, the sequels cemented Jamie's status as one of Hollywood's leading men. One of Jamie Dornan's career turning points was the "Fifty Shades" trilogy. It made him a global celebrity, but it also presented a challenge as he had to deal with the intricacies of notoriety and public opinion. In the end, his dedication to his work and his poise in the limelight enabled him to come out of the "Fifty Shades" frenzy not just as a box office success but also as a reputable and adaptable actor prepared to take on new and varied tasks.

CHAPTER FOUR

Acting Challenges and Diverse Roles Beyond Christian Grey

Following the "Fifty Shades" frenzy, Jamie Dornan found himself at a fork in the road. Although the series had made him a household name throughout the globe, it also carried the risk of stereotyping him as the stolid millionaire Christian Grey. Jamie set out on a quest to investigate a variety of roles and acting difficulties to demonstrate his breadth and prevent creative stagnation. He played Czechoslovakian soldier Jan Kubiš in the 2018 war drama "Anthropoid," which was about his mission to kill Nazi chief Reinhard Heydrich. He was able to discard his contemporary character and explore the complexity of a man juggling moral uncertainty and wartime duty in this historical drama.

In the film "A Private War," he played the courageous war journalist Marie Colvin, a photographer who was devoted to recording scenes in warfare. Her job was no less demanding. Jamie transformed both physically and emotionally to capture the power and tenderness of Colvin; his performance was praised by critics for being honest and moving. Jamie continued to embrace diversity by starring in the independent films "Endings, Beginnings" and "Wild Mountain Thyme." The former, a semi-improvised romantic drama, allowed him to experiment with his comedic timing and showcase his lighter side. The latter, a whimsical Irish love story, saw him return to his roots, speaking his native accent and capturing the charm and humor of rural Ireland.

He explored the sci-fi thriller genre in "Synchronic," playing a paramedic haunted by the mysterious deaths of time-traveling clients. This role demanded physicality and emotional depth, showcasing Jamie's ability to navigate suspenseful storylines and portray characters struggling with loss and existential questions. In 2020, he teamed up with Kenneth Branagh for the critically acclaimed semi-autobiographical drama "Belfast." Set against the backdrop of The Troubles in Northern Ireland, the film resonated deeply with Jamie, who drew on his own childhood experiences to deliver a moving and authentic performance.

More recently, he starred in the quirky comedy "Barb and Star Go to Vista Del Mar" and the critically acclaimed miniseries "The Tourist." The former allowed him to embrace his comedic talents, while the latter saw him tackle a complex mystery thriller role, demanding a nuanced portrayal of a man with amnesia grappling with his identity. Throughout his post-"Fifty Shades" career, Jamie actively sought out projects that pushed him outside his comfort zone. He challenged himself with diverse accents, explored complex emotional states, and navigated genres ranging from historical drama to science fiction. He proved his commitment to artistic integrity, refusing to be defined by his past success and continually seeking new ways to grow as an actor.

CHAPTER FIVE

Love, Family, and Personal Life: Balancing Stardom with Privacy

While Jamie Dornan's professional life often plays out in the public eye, he fiercely guards his personal life, valuing privacy for himself and his family. In 2010, he met English actress and musician Amelia Warner, and it was love at first sight. They kept their relationship relatively private, but their connection deepened quickly, leading to an engagement in 2012 and a wedding in 2013. Amelia, known for her musical career and involvement in film scores, proved to be a grounding force for Jamie, offering love, support, and a safe haven away from the spotlight. They welcomed their first daughter, Dulcie, in 2013, followed by Elva in 2016 and Alberta in 2019. Fatherhood brought immense joy to Jamie, who embraced his role with dedication and love. He often speaks of the importance of family and how prioritizing his children grounds him and provides perspective amidst the chaos of Hollywood.

Despite balancing work with fatherhood, Jamie remains deeply committed to his wife. They are rarely seen at high-profile events together, preferring to cherish their privacy and nurture their relationship behind closed doors. Their mutual respect, shared values, and understanding of each other's careers have contributed to the longevity and strength of their partnership. While Jamie values his privacy, he doesn't shy away from speaking about his passions outside of acting. He is a skilled musician, playing guitar and piano, and often writes his own music. He enjoys rugby and remains a loyal supporter of his hometown team, the Belfast Harlequins. He also actively supports various charities and humanitarian causes, showcasing his compassion and desire to make a positive impact on the world.

Maintaining a balance between stardom and personal life can be challenging, but Jamie navigates it with grace and integrity. He remains selective about interviews and social media presence, avoiding overexposure and protecting his family. He is conscious of the media's tendency to create narratives around his life, choosing instead to share only what he deems comfortable and necessary.

Despite the inevitable intrusion of fame, Jamie has managed to carve out a private space for himself and his loved ones. He prioritizes time with his family, cherishes simple moments, and pursues his personal interests outside of the limelight. This dedication to his personal life contributes to his grounded nature and authentic performances on screen.

Jamie Dornan's Wife

Jamie Dornan, the charismatic actor known for his roles in "Fifty Shades of Grey" and "Belfast," has been happily married to the talented and versatile Amelia Warner since 2013. But who is the woman who captured the heart of one of Hollywood's most sought-after actors?

From Acting to Music: A Creative Journey

Amelia Warner was born in London, England, in 1982. Her artistic inclinations emerged early on, and she began acting at a young age. She landed her first major role in the 2000 BBC adaptation of "Lorna Doone," followed by appearances in films like "Mansfield Park" and "Aeolus." While acting provided her with a platform to showcase her talent, Amelia's true passion lay in music. She gradually transitioned into composing soundtracks for films and television shows, including "Nowhere Boy" and "The Musketeers." Her haunting melodies and evocative compositions garnered critical acclaim, establishing her as a rising star in the world of music composition.

Finding Love with Jamie Dornan

Amelia and Jamie's paths crossed in 2010, and their connection was instant. They quickly fell in love and were married in a private ceremony in 2013. Since then, they have built a beautiful life together, raising three daughters and supporting each other's creative endeavors.

A Supportive and Private Partner

While Jamie Dornan enjoys the spotlight, Amelia prefers to keep her personal life private. However, she is often seen by his side at red-carpet events and industry gatherings, offering him unwavering support and radiating warmth with her genuine smile. Their relationship is built on mutual respect, love, and a shared appreciation for each other's talents.

Beyond the Spotlight: A Life of Passion and Purpose

Despite her connection to Hollywood, Amelia maintains a grounded and authentic lifestyle. She is passionate about environmental causes and actively supports organizations that promote sustainability and conservation. She also continues to pursue her music career, releasing solo albums and collaborating with other artists.

A Multifaceted Talent: Musician, Composer, and More

Amelia Warner is not just Jamie Dornan's wife; she is a talented individual in her own right. Her career spans acting, music composition, and songwriting, showcasing her diverse skills and artistic expression. Her quiet strength, creative spirit, and unwavering support for her husband make her an inspiration to many.

Jamie Dornan Kids

Jamie Dornan, the heartthrob actor known for his captivating performances in films like "Fifty Shades of Grey" and "Belfast," is much more than just a movie star. He is also a devoted father to his three daughters, Dulcie, Elva, and Alberta. While he fiercely protects their privacy, glimpses into their family life reveal a heartwarming picture of love, laughter, and genuine connection.

Welcoming the Firstborns: Dulcie and Elva

Jamie and his wife, musician and composer Amelia Warner, welcomed their first daughter, Dulcie, in 2013.

Two years later, their family grew with the arrival of Elva in 2015. While details about their early childhood remain guarded, glimpses through public appearances and interviews offer a peek into their personalities.

Jamie Dornan and Dulcie

Dulcie, the eldest, is described as having inherited her father's mischievous charm and her mother's artistic sensibilities. In a 2020 interview with "People," Jamie revealed that Dulcie, at the age of seven, had already begun developing her musical talent, much like her mother. Elva, on the other hand, is known for her energetic spirit and bubbly personality. Sharing a photo of her on his Instagram in 2022, Jamie lovingly captioned it, "My little firecracker turns 7 today. Love you to the moon and back, Elva."

The Arrival of Little Alberta:

In 2019, the Dornan family expanded further with the birth of their third daughter, Alberta. Unlike her older sisters, Alberta has largely remained out of the public eye, with Jamie and Amelia opting to keep her life even more private. However, Amelia posted a picture of their three daughters—three pairs of shoes—on Instagram on Mother's Day 2019, captioning it, "So proud of these three wonderful girls, it's an honor being their mum.. feeling incredibly lucky today #happymothersday."

Raising Daughters with Love and Protection:

Jamie and Amelia prioritize their daughters' privacy and well-being above all else. They rarely share their daughters' faces on social media and strive to provide them with a normal childhood despite their parents' fame. In an interview with "The Times" in 2021, Jamie expressed his desire for his daughters to have a sense of normalcy, saying, "I just want them to have a regular life."

Despite their busy schedules, Jamie and Amelia make time for their daughters, participating in activities like family outings, and holidays, and simply spending quality time together. In a 2020 interview with "People," Jamie spoke about the joys of fatherhood, saying, "It's been the greatest thing in my life."

A Balancing Act: Fame and Family Life

Balancing a demanding career with fatherhood is no easy feat, and Jamie has spoken openly about the challenges he faces. In a 2023 interview with "GQ," he admitted, "There are times when I feel guilty about being away from them." However, he also emphasizes the importance of setting boundaries and making time for his family.

CHAPTER SIX

Philanthropy and Advocacy: Using Influence for Good

Beyond his captivating performances and charming persona, Jamie Dornan possesses a deep-seated desire to contribute to the greater good. He leverages his platform and influence to support various charitable causes and advocate for issues close to his heart, demonstrating his commitment to social responsibility and positive change.

Championing Children's Rights:

As a father of three daughters, Jamie holds a special place in his heart for children's well-being. He is a dedicated supporter of UNICEF, the United Nations Children's Fund, which advocates for the rights and protection of children worldwide. He has participated in fundraising initiatives and awareness campaigns, using his voice to champion access to education, healthcare, and safety for all children.

Raising Awareness for Mental Health:

Jamie openly acknowledges his struggles with mental health, particularly anxiety, and uses his platform to normalize conversations about mental well-being. He actively supports Mind, a leading mental health charity in the UK, encouraging individuals to seek help and break down the stigma surrounding mental health issues. He has participated in fundraising events and public campaigns, promoting open dialogue and access to mental health resources.

Standing Up for Refugees:

The plight of refugees and displaced people resonates deeply with Jamie, whose hometown of Belfast witnessed firsthand the struggles of conflict and displacement. He collaborates with the International Rescue Committee (IRC), a global humanitarian organization that assists refugees and migrants. He has visited refugee camps, met with individuals affected by displacement, and participated in fundraising efforts, raising awareness about the challenges faced by refugees and advocating for their rights.

Environmental Advocacy:

As an avid outdoorsman and nature enthusiast, Jamie champions environmental causes and sustainable practices. He supports organizations like Greenpeace, which works to protect the environment and promote ecological sustainability. He advocates for responsible consumerism, raising awareness about the impact of climate change and encouraging individuals to adopt eco-friendly habits.

Beyond Traditional Philanthropy:

Jamie Dornan's commitment to social good extends beyond financial contributions and public appearances. He actively lends his name and voice to campaigns, participates in awareness-raising events, and uses his social media platforms to advocate for the causes he believes in. He encourages his fans to get involved, supporting organizations and initiatives that address various social and environmental challenges.

CHAPTER SEVEN

Facing Scrutiny and Overcoming Obstacles: Maintaining Integrity

The path to success is rarely paved with smooth stones, and Jamie Dornan's journey is no exception. Throughout his career, he has faced various challenges and navigated his fair share of scrutiny, both personal and professional. However, his ability to overcome obstacles and maintain integrity has solidified his position as a respected and admired figure in the entertainment industry.

Navigating the "Fifty Shades" Phenomenon:

The immense success of the "Fifty Shades" franchise brought Jamie Dornan global recognition but also intense scrutiny. The sexually explicit nature of the films and the character of Christian Grey sparked debate and criticism, with some questioning his decision to take on such a controversial role. Jamie faced accusations of perpetuating harmful stereotypes and criticism for the film's portrayal of BDSM relationships. However, he handled the criticism with grace and professionalism. He defended his artistic choices while acknowledging the film's potential to trigger sensitive viewers. He emphasized the importance of individual interpretation and avoided engaging in heated debates. By maintaining his composure and refusing to be drawn into negativity, he preserved his dignity and garnered respect from both fans and critics.

Challenges of Fame and Media Scrutiny:

The spotlight of fame can be a double-edged sword, and Jamie has experienced its challenges firsthand. He has been subjected to tabloid rumors and paparazzi intrusion, facing unwanted attention to his personal life and relationships. He has learned to navigate the media landscape cautiously, choosing to share only what he deems necessary and maintaining a healthy distance from the constant scrutiny.

Staying True to His Artistic Values:

While commercial success is undoubtedly important, Jamie has consistently prioritized artistic integrity over box office numbers. He has actively sought out diverse roles that challenge him as an actor and allow him to explore different facets of his craft. He has embraced independent films and taken on projects that resonate with him personally, even if they lacked the mainstream appeal of bigger productions. This dedication to artistic exploration has earned him critical acclaim and the respect of his peers. He has proven himself to be a versatile actor capable of portraying complex characters and delivering nuanced performances. His willingness to step outside his comfort zone and take creative risks has established him as a serious and respected artist, not just a Hollywood heartthrob.

Overcoming Personal Challenges:

Like everyone else, Jamie has faced personal challenges and setbacks. He has openly acknowledged his struggles with anxiety and the pressures of fame. He has also spoken about the loss of his mother and the impact it had on his life. By sharing his vulnerabilities and experiences, he has connected with his audience on a deeper level and inspired others to embrace their own imperfections.

Finding Strength in Resilience:

Throughout his career, Jamie has consistently demonstrated resilience in the face of adversity. He has not allowed criticism, scrutiny, or personal challenges to define him. He has used them as opportunities to grow and evolve, emerging stronger and more determined to achieve his goals. His ability to bounce back from setbacks and persevere through difficult times is a testament to his character and unwavering work ethic.

CHAPTER EIGHT

Post-Fifty Shades: Reclaiming his narrative and artistic freedom

The "Fifty Shades" franchise catapulted Jamie Dornan to global fame, forever etching the image of Christian Grey in the minds of audiences worldwide. While the success was undeniable, it also carried the burden of typecasting and the risk of being defined solely by that one character. However, with a deliberate and strategic approach, Jamie embarked on a journey to reclaim his narrative and explore the vastness of his artistic potential.

Seeking Diverse Roles and Stepping Outside Comfort Zones:

Conscious of the typecasting potential, Jamie actively sought roles that showcased his versatility and challenged him as an actor. He delved into independent films like "Anthropoid" and "Endings, Beginnings," shedding the polished persona of Christian Grey and immersing himself in complex characters with raw emotions and diverse accents. He embraced comedic roles in "Barb and Star Go to Vista Del Mar" and "Wild Mountain Thyme," proving his ability to deliver humor and charm alongside his dramatic gravitas.

Collaborating with Renowned Directors and Artists:

To further elevate his artistic profile, Jamie collaborated with acclaimed directors and artists. He starred in Kenneth Branagh's semi-autobiographical film "Belfast," capturing the nuances of growing up during The Troubles in Northern Ireland. He worked with David Cronenberg on the psychological thriller "Synchronic," exploring themes of time travel and loss. These collaborations exposed him to different filmmaking styles and honed his craft under the guidance of established masters.

Exploring Sensitive and Socially Relevant Themes:

Beyond individual characters, Jamie gravitated toward projects that tackled societal issues. He portrayed a journalist struggling with trauma in "A Private War," highlighting the dangers faced by war correspondents. He played a man with amnesia confronting his identity in "The Tourist," raising questions about trust and perception. These roles allowed him to contribute to conversations about important topics while showcasing his ability to navigate complex narratives.

Embracing Theatre and Returning to His Roots:

In 2023, Jamie returned to the stage with a leading role in a new production of Harold Pinter's "Betrayal." Stepping back onto the boards reconnected him with his theatrical roots and allowed him to explore the intimacy and immediacy of live performance. This return to theatre demonstrated his commitment to his craft and his desire to constantly challenge himself artistically.

Reclaiming the Narrative and Evolving as an Artist:

Through his post-"Fifty Shades" choices, Jamie successfully steered his career away from typecasting. He showcased his range, tackled diverse roles, and collaborated with acclaimed talents, solidifying his reputation as a versatile and committed actor. His willingness to explore sensitive themes and his return to theatre further cemented his artistry and his desire to contribute meaningfully to the entertainment industry.

Looking Ahead:

Jamie Dornan's post-Fifty Shades" journey is a testament to his dedication to growth and artistic exploration. He has defied expectations, reclaimed his narrative, and established himself as a force to be reckoned with in the world of acting. Looking ahead, his trajectory promises even more diverse and captivating performances, solidifying his position as a talented and respected artist with a long and exciting Dornan's artistic hunger extending beyond the realm of acting. In recent years, he has ventured into the world of producing and directing, taking control of his creative vision and expanding his footprint in the entertainment industry.

Stepping Behind the Camera:

Driven by a desire for greater creative autonomy and a deeper understanding of the filmmaking process, Jamie began exploring producing opportunities. His first foray came in 2018 with the historical thriller "Terminal," where he served as both star and executive producer. This experience allowed him to influence the film's direction, collaborate with filmmakers on a broader level, and gain valuable insights into the production process.

Directing His First Short Film:

In 2021, Jamie took a bold leap by directing his first short film, "Hiatus." This black-and-white psychological drama showcased his ability to translate his artistic vision into a compelling narrative, exploring themes of isolation and self-discovery. The film received positive reviews and critical acclaim, highlighting his potential as a director and storyteller.

Pursuing Film Projects with Passion:

Fueled by his initial success, Jamie has actively sought out producing opportunities for films that resonate with him. He co-founded "The Unraveling," a production company dedicated to developing and producing independent films with a focus on quality storytelling and artistic merit. This venture allows him to champion projects he believes in and collaborate with talented filmmakers who share his vision.

Balancing Acting and Directing:

While directing holds a growing appeal, Jamie remains committed to his acting career. He carefully navigates the dual roles, ensuring each project receives his full dedication and attention. He recognizes the challenges of balancing these demanding pursuits, but he relishes the opportunity to learn and grow as an artist in different creative capacities.

Exploring Diverse Genres and Stories:

Jamie's producing and directing aspirations are not confined to a single genre. He is drawn to stories with emotional depth, complex characters, and thought-provoking themes. He is currently attached to produce and star in "Heart of Stone," a Cold War spy thriller, showcasing his versatility and interest in exploring diverse cinematic territories.

The Future of Jamie Dornan's Creative Endeavors:

Jamie Dornan's journey as a producer and director is still unfolding, but his initial ventures have already demonstrated his potential and passion for shaping narratives behind the camera. As he continues to hone his skills and collaborate with talented individuals, his creative footprint is sure to expand, paving the way for exciting and impactful projects in the years to come.ng career ahead.

CHAPTER NINE

Producing and Directing: Expanding his creative footprint

Jamie Dornan's artistic hunger extends beyond the realm of acting. In recent years, he has ventured into the world of producing and directing, taking control of his creative vision and expanding his footprint in the entertainment industry. Driven by a desire for greater creative autonomy and a deeper understanding of the filmmaking process, Jamie began exploring producing opportunities. His first foray came in 2018 with the historical thriller "Terminal," where he served as both star and executive producer. This experience allowed him to influence the film's direction, collaborate with filmmakers on a broader level, and gain valuable insights into the production process.

Directing His First Short Film:

In 2021, Jamie took a bold leap by directing his first short film, "Hiatus." This black-and-white psychological drama showcased his ability to translate his artistic vision into a compelling narrative, exploring themes of isolation and self-discovery. The film received positive reviews and critical acclaim, highlighting his potential as a director and storyteller.

Pursuing Film Projects with Passion:

Fueled by his initial success, Jamie has actively sought out producing opportunities for films that resonate with him. He co-founded "The Unraveling," a production company dedicated to developing and producing independent films with a focus on quality storytelling and artistic merit. This venture allows him to champion projects he believes in and collaborate with talented filmmakers who share his vision.

Balancing Acting and Directing:

While directing holds a growing appeal, Jamie remains committed to his acting career. He carefully navigates the dual roles, ensuring each project receives his full dedication and attention. He recognizes the challenges of balancing these demanding pursuits, but he relishes the opportunity to learn and grow as an artist in different creative capacities.

Exploring Diverse Genres and Stories:

Jamie's producing and directing aspirations are not confined to a single genre. He is drawn to stories with emotional depth, complex characters, and thought-provoking themes. He is currently attached to produce and star in "Heart of Stone," a Cold War spy thriller, showcasing his versatility and interest in exploring diverse cinematic territories.

The Future of Jamie Dornan's Creative Endeavors:

Jamie Dornan's journey as a producer and director is still unfolding, but his initial ventures have already demonstrated his potential and passion for shaping narratives behind the camera. As he continues to hone his skills and collaborate with talented individuals, his creative footprint is sure to expand, paving the way for exciting and impactful projects in the years to come.

Reflecting on Success and Facing the Future: Legacy and Aspirations

As the curtain closes on this exploration of Jamie Dornan's remarkable journey, we arrive at a poignant crossroads: reflecting on the legacy he has carved and gazing toward the uncharted horizon of his aspirations.

Beyond the Shadow of Christian Grey:

While "Fifty Shades of Grey" propelled Jamie Dornan to global fame, his impact transcends the mere box office figures and fleeting media frenzy. He has meticulously crafted a legacy that extends far beyond the enigmatic billionaire persona that first introduced him to the world. His artistry lies in his transformative ability to embody diverse characters, his unwavering commitment to pushing his creative boundaries, and his dedication to storytelling that resonates with emotional depth and complexity.

A Tapestry of Artistic Evolution:

Dornan's post-Fifty Shades" filmography paints a vibrant tapestry of artistic evolution. From the raw intensity of a war correspondent in "A Private War" to the introspective vulnerability of a man grappling with amnesia in "The Tourist," he has fearlessly navigated genres and embraced challenging roles. His willingness to collaborate with esteemed directors like Kenneth Branagh in "Belfast" and David Cronenberg in

"Synchronic" further cements his artistic integrity and thirst for creative exploration.

A Champion for Humanity:

Dornan's impact extends beyond the silver screen. He has leveraged his platform to champion issues close to his heart, becoming a powerful voice for underprivileged communities and marginalized individuals. His dedication to children's rights through UNICEF, his support for mental health awareness with Mind, and his advocacy for refugees with the International Rescue Committee showcase his unwavering commitment to using his influence for positive social change.

Fueling Aspirations, Inspiring Generations:

Jamie Dornan's journey serves as a beacon of inspiration for aspiring actors and artists worldwide. His relentless work ethic, his resilience in the face of challenges, and his unwavering dedication to his craft offer valuable lessons about pursuing artistic dreams with integrity and authenticity. He embodies the courage to take risks, the wisdom to learn from setbacks, and the humility to remain grounded despite achieving incredible success.

A Glimpse into the Future:

Gazing into the future, the possibilities for Jamie Dornan's career are as vast as his ambition. His burgeoning interest in producing and directing, evident in his co-founding of "The Unraveling" and his debut short film "Hiatus," hints at a desire for greater creative control and storytelling exploration. This foray into filmmaking, coupled with his acting prowess, promises a diverse and exciting future where his artistic potential can flourish unhindered.

A Legacy Etched in Creativity and Compassion:

Ultimately, Jamie Dornan's legacy will be defined not just by his on-screen performances or box office accolades, but by the indelible mark he leaves on the world through his artistry, his integrity, and his unwavering commitment to making a difference. He is an artist who challenges himself and entertains audiences, a humanitarian who advocates for marginalized voices, and an inspiration who empowers aspiring talents. As his journey continues to unfold, one thing remains certain: the future holds boundless possibilities for this multifaceted artist, whose legacy is forever etched in creativity and compassion.

The Man Behind the Image: A Portrait of Jamie Dornan Jamie Dornan, the name conjures images of smoldering good looks, captivating onscreen presence, and the enigmatic billionaire Christian Grey. But to simply define him by these facets would be a grave disservice to the complex and multifaceted individual who resides beneath the surface. This chapter delves deeper, peeling back the layers of the image to reveal the man behind it, the values that shape him, and the passions that fuel his journey.

Music: A Sanctuary of the Soul:

Music has always been a refuge for Jamie, a space where he can express himself authentically and connect with his emotions on a deeper level. His musical prowess extends beyond mere appreciation; he is a skilled guitarist and pianist, often composing his own melodies and lyrics. This creative outlet serves as a personal sanctuary, allowing him to explore vulnerabilities and process experiences in a way that transcends the public eye.

Beyond the Spotlight: Embracing a Balanced Life:

Despite the undeniable allure of his career, Jamie fiercely protects his privacy, prioritizing a sense of normalcy in his personal life. He cherishes quiet moments with his wife Amelia Warner, a musician and actress, and their three daughters. The family remains at the heart of his world, offering him grounding and joy outside the whirlwind of Hollywood. He regularly escapes to the outdoors, finding solace in hiking, rugby, and other activities that reconnect him with his roots and recharge his spirit.

Facing Challenges with Grace and Vulnerability:

Jamie doesn't shy away from acknowledging the darker aspects of life. He has openly spoken about his struggles with anxiety, highlighting the pressures of fame and the importance of mental health awareness. His willingness to share his vulnerabilities resonates deeply with audiences, inspiring empathy and encouraging open conversations about often stigmatized issues. His ability to overcome hurdles with grace and resilience has earned him respect and admiration, demonstrating that strength lies not in the absence of struggle, but in the courage to confront it.

Standing by His Values: Integrity and Social Responsibility:

Integrity and authenticity are cornerstones of Jamie's character. He aligns himself with projects that resonate with his values, using his platform to advocate for causes he believes in. He is a dedicated supporter of UNICEF, raising awareness for children's rights and advocating for their well-being. He actively supports Mind, a mental health charity, encouraging open dialogues and access to mental health resources. His commitment to social responsibility extends to environmental causes, collaborating with organizations like Greenpeace to promote sustainable practices. These endeavors showcase his genuine desire to make a positive impact beyond the entertainment industry.

Evolution and Aspiration: Looking Beyond the Horizon:

Jamie's artistic journey is a testament to his constant evolution. He actively seeks diverse roles that challenge him creatively, refusing to be typecast or confined to a single genre. His foray into independent films like "Anthropoid" and "Endings, Beginnings" showcased his dramatic range, while his comedic turns in "Barb and Star Go to Vista Del Mar" and "Wild Mountain Thyme" highlighted his versatility and charm. His recent return to the stage with a leading role in "Betrayal" reaffirmed his commitment to theatre and his love for live performance. Beyond acting, Jamie has ventured into producing and directing, co-founding "The Unraveling" to develop independent films with artistic merit. His debut short film, "Hiatus," showcased his directorial vision and storytelling talent. This burgeoning interest in filmmaking opens exciting possibilities for the future, allowing him to express his artistry in multifaceted ways.

A Legacy Etched in Creativity and Compassion:

Jamie Dornan's legacy will extend far beyond box office figures or celebrity stardom. He is an artist who pushes boundaries, a voice for the unheard, and an advocate for positive change. His dedication to storytelling, his unwavering commitment to his values, and his genuine connection with his audience ensure that his impact will resonate for years to come. He is a reminder that success can be measured not just by achievements, but by the lasting impact one leaves on the world around them.

Jamie Dornan was rushed to the hospital with symptoms of a heart attack after coming into contact with toxic caterpillars

Jamie Dornan, star of Fifty Shades of Grey, was recently taken to the hospital with signs of a heart attack after an encounter with deadly caterpillars while on a golf vacation in Portugal. Jamie's friend Gordon Smart, who accompanied the actor on the March 2023 trip, revealed during an episode of BBC's "The Good, the Bad, and the Unexpected" podcast, "It turns out that there are caterpillars on the golf courses in the south of Portugal that have been killing people's dogs and giving men in their the forties heart attacks."

After spending the night out with Jamie, 41, and two other pals, the 43-year-old Scottish broadcaster said that he felt "tingling" in his left hand and arm and knew right away that his symptoms were "the sign of the start of a heart attack." A heart rate of 210 BPM, which is much higher than the average of 60 to 100 BPM, was also recorded by him. "Although I'm a pretty healthy guy, you're certain that you're convincing yourself that you're having a heart attack once you start thinking you're having one," Gordon said. Gordon recalled waking up in a hospital bed after passing out in an Uber on the way to the ER, and he saw a fellow traveler being carried past with identical symptoms right away. Gordon said that soon after being released from the hospital, Jamie's symptoms became worse and that he too had to be sent to the emergency department for treatment. My left arm, left leg, and right leg all became numb around twenty minutes after you departed, Gordon. "And I ended up in the rear of an ambulance," he remembered Jamie saying to him. A week or so later, Gordon said that the story took an intriguing turn, even though he and his pals made a full recovery from the unexplained occurrence.

Gordon said that soon after the friends got back from their vacation, he received a call from a doctor, who was probably the one who had treated the companions for their illnesses. The doctor asked Gordon whether the group had encountered caterpillars while out golfing.

The doctor stated that people may get symptoms similar to their own by brushing up against a natural kind of pine processionary moth caterpillar.

According to Forest Research, handling caterpillars may result in symptoms ranging from mild skin and eye irritation to more severe allergic responses. The insects can be a "hazard to human and animal health."

A local gardener who came into touch with the caterpillars' deadly hairs reportedly had four heart attacks as a result of anaphylactic shock, according to an article published in The Portugal News in February 2016. According to the publication, the man's body responded to the insects fatally, necessitating triple bypass surgery.

Gordon wrapped up his strange story with, "It turns out we brushed up against processionary caterpillars and had been very lucky to come out of that one alive."

Treatment and Recovery:

Thankfully, Dornan and Smart received prompt medical attention and made a full recovery. Dornan confirmed on the Jonathan Ross Show that he spent "a good few hours" in the hospital but was "absolutely fine" afterward. The incident served as a reminder of the potential dangers of encountering wildlife, even in seemingly mundane situations like a golf course. It also highlighted the importance of seeking medical attention if experiencing unusual symptoms, especially after potential exposure to allergens.

Current Health Status:

As of January 24, 2024, there are no publicly reported health concerns for Jamie Dornan. He continues to work on upcoming projects, including the spy thriller "Heart of Stone" and the horror film "A Haunting in Venice." Based on public appearances and social media activity, Dornan appears to be healthy and active.

Dornan movies and TV shows

Jamie Dornan's career has taken him from the runways of Milan to the silver screen of Hollywood, captivating audiences with his charisma, versatility, and dedication to his craft. This comprehensive filmography explores his journey through both film and television, showcasing the diverse roles he has embodied and the evolution of his artistry.

Early Beginnings: Stepping into the Spotlight (2006-2011)

- Marie Antoinette (2006): Dornan made his film debut as Count Axel Fersen in Sofia Coppola's opulent historical drama, showcasing his early screen presence and charm.

- X-Men Origins: Wolverine (2009): A small but memorable role as Kyle, highlighting his action-hero potential.
- Once Upon a Time (2011): His portrayal of Sheriff Graham/Huntsman in the ABC fantasy series garnered attention and established him as a rising star.

Breakthrough and Beyond: Exploring Diverse Genres (2013-2018)

- The Fall (2013-2016): This critically acclaimed BBC series catapulted Dornan to international fame as Paul Spector, a charming yet deranged serial killer. His nuanced performance showcased his ability to portray complex and challenging characters.
- Fifty Shades of Grey (2015), Fifty Shades Darker (2017), and Fifty Shades Freed (2018): The commercially successful "Fifty Shades" trilogy solidified Dornan's global recognition as the enigmatic billionaire Christian Grey. While the films sparked debate, his commitment to the role

proved his commercial viability and willingness to take on controversial projects.
- Anthropoid (2016): Dornan delivered a powerful performance as Jan Kubiš, a Czechoslovakian resistance fighter, showcasing his versatility and dramatic range.
- The Siege of Jadotville (2016): He portrayed Commandant Pat Quinlan, leading a courageous stand against overwhelming odds in this historical war film.
- A Private War (2018): Dornan embodied the real-life war correspondent Paul Conroy, demonstrating his commitment to portraying impactful stories and complex individuals.

Post-"Fifty Shades": Reclaiming his Narrative and Artistic Freedom (2019-Present)

- Terminal (2018): Serving as both star and executive producer, Dornan explored the thriller genre with this gritty tale of two hitmen.
- Synchronic (2019): Stepping into the realm of science fiction, he played a paramedic grappling

with a mysterious drug and its time-altering effects.
- Death and Nightingales (2018): Dornan ventured into miniseries with this Irish drama, portraying Liam Ward, a man caught in a web of family secrets and violence.
- Robin Hood (2018): His take on the iconic outlaw in this action-packed film offered a modern twist on the classic character.
- My Dinner with Hervé (2018): Dornan delivered a comedic turn as Danny Tate, a journalist interviewing the eccentric entertainer Hervé Villechaize.
- Barb and Star Go to Vista Del Mar (2021): Embracing his comedic talents, he played Edgar Pagét, a flamboyant villain in this quirky and hilarious film.
- Wild Mountain Thyme (2020): A romantic comedy featuring Dornan alongside Emily Blunt, showcasing his charm and romantic leading man potential.

- Trolls World Tour (2020): Dornan lent his voice to the character of Chaz in this animated film, demonstrating his vocal talents and versatility.
- Endings, Beginnings (2019): He portrayed Jack, a complex character navigating love and loss in this romantic drama.
- Belfast (2021): Dornan delivered a heartfelt performance as Pa, a father protecting his family during The Troubles in Kenneth Branagh's semi-autobiographical film. He received a Golden Globe nomination for Best Supporting Actor – Motion Picture for his role.
- Heart of Stone (2023): This upcoming Cold War spy thriller marks Dornan's co-starring and producing debut, showcasing his expanding career ambitions.

Television Return: Expanding his Horizons (2022-Present)

- The Tourist (2022-present): Dornan stars as Elliot Stanley/Eugene Cassidy, a man with amnesia searching for his identity in this suspenseful miniseries. His performance has garnered critical

acclaim, highlighting his talent in carrying both dramatic and comedic elements.
- A Haunting in Venice (2023): He portrayed Dr. Leslie Ferrier in this Agatha Christie adaptation, further demonstrating his range and interest in diverse projects.

Jamie Dornan's Salary and Net Worth

Jamie Dornan, the Irish actor who rose to international fame with his portrayal of the enigmatic billionaire Christian Grey in the "Fifty Shades" trilogy, has captivated audiences with his talent and charm. But beyond the silver screen, there's a natural curiosity about his financial standing. So, let's delve into the world of Jamie Dornan's net worth and salary, separating facts from speculation.

Estimating Net Worth: A Varied Landscape

As of October 27, 2023, estimates for Jamie Dornan's net worth vary slightly depending on the source:

- Celebrity Net Worth: Their website pegs it at $18 million.

- Things: An article published in January 2024 places it between $14 and $15 million, referencing other sources.
- Market Realist: They state a net worth of $14 million in a January 2024 article, citing Celebrity Net Worth.

While the exact figure might fluctuate, considering the range provided by reputable sources, $18 million seems to be the most commonly cited estimate.

Unpacking the Salary Enigma:

Actor salaries are notoriously confidential and depend on various factors, including project budget, negotiation power, and industry norms. While specific details remain under wraps, some insights can be gleaned from reported figures for specific roles:

- Fifty Shades of Grey: Dornan reportedly received $250,000 for the first film, but his salary soared for the sequels. Some sources estimate around $5.6 million for "Fifty Shades Darker" and "Fifty Shades Freed."
- Belfast: Dornan co-produced and starred in this acclaimed film, likely earning a combination of

acting fees and producer profits. Specific figures remain undisclosed.
- Recent projects: Information about his salary for recent works like "Heart of Stone" and "The Tourist" is limited.

A Glimpse into the Future:

With a successful acting career, recent forays into producing, and a commitment to his craft, Jamie Dornan's financial future appears bright. His talent, coupled with his business acumen, promises continued growth and success. While the exact figures surrounding his net worth and salary might remain elusive, one thing is certain: Jamie Dornan has established himself as a force to be reckoned with in the entertainment industry.

Jamie Dornan's Fifty Shades Salary: From a Modest Sum to Millions

Jamie Dornan's portrayal of the enigmatic billionaire Christian Grey in the "Fifty Shades" trilogy propelled him to international fame and fortune. But how much did he earn for taking on this iconic role? Let's delve into the facts surrounding his "Fifty Shades" salary, separating myths from reality.

Early Days: A Starting Point with Room to Grow

Indeed, Dornan's initial salary for the first "Fifty Shades of Grey" film was relatively modest. He reportedly received $250,000, a figure considered standard for actors of his caliber at the time, especially for a film with an uncertain box office fate.

However, the producers had negotiated a "franchise deal" with Dornan, meaning his salary would increase significantly for the sequels if the first film became a success. And that's exactly what happened.

Box Office Boom and Soaring Salaries

"Fifty Shades of Grey" smashed box office records, grossing over $570 million worldwide. This commercial success triggered the predetermined salary increase for Dornan in the subsequent films. According to various sources, he earned:

- $2.5 million for "Fifty Shades Darker" (2017)
- $5.4 million for "Fifty Shades Freed" (2018)

This represents a massive increase from his initial fee, showcasing the power of box office performance and pre-negotiated contracts.

Beyond the Numbers: Additional Considerations

It's important to remember that these figures may not represent the full picture:

- Profit-sharing: Some reports suggest that Dornan may have negotiated a profit-sharing deal, meaning he could have earned additional income based on the films' overall profitability.
- Endorsements and other opportunities: The "Fifty Shades" franchise's success likely opened doors for Dornan to secure lucrative endorsement deals and other opportunities, further boosting his overall earnings.

A Springboard to Bigger Things

The "Fifty Shades" franchise undoubtedly had a significant impact on Dornan's career and finances. It not only brought him global recognition but also opened doors to bigger and more diverse projects. He has since starred in acclaimed films like "Belfast" and "Barb and Star Go to Vista Del Mar," showcasing his range and talent beyond the "Fifty Shades" persona.

Jamie Dornan Charms the Audience on The Late Late Show: A Hilarious and Heartfelt Visit

Jamie Dornan, the dashing Irish actor known for his captivating performances in "Fifty Shades of Grey" and "Belfast," made a memorable appearance on Ireland's beloved late-night talk show, "The Late Late Show," hosted by Ryan Tubridy, on Friday, October 27, 2023. The episode was filled with laughter, heartwarming stories, and a glimpse into Dornan's life beyond the silver screen.

A Hilarious Start with a Musical Challenge:

Dornan's visit began with a lighthearted challenge. Tubridy presented him with a medley of Irish pop songs, asking him to sing along. Dornan, known for his self-deprecating humor, readily embraced the challenge, even attempting some impromptu dance moves, much to the audience's amusement.

Jamie Dornan on The Late Late Show: A Dashing Blend of Charm, Heartfelt Moments, and Irish Craic

Jamie Dornan, the charismatic Northern Irish actor, has graced the stage of The Late Late Show on several occasions, each visit leaving a lasting impression on viewers. His appearances have been a delightful mix of wit, insightful conversations, and moments of genuine vulnerability, all delivered with his signature Irish charm.

Dornan's most recent appearance, in October 2022, was particularly poignant. Promoting his acclaimed film "Belfast," he opened up about the personal connection to the story, set against the backdrop of The Troubles in Northern Ireland. He spoke candidly about the loss of his father during filming, adding an emotional layer to the interview that resonated deeply with the audience. Host Ryan Tubridy skillfully navigated the conversation, allowing Dornan to share his grief while celebrating the film's success and its connection to his roots.

Yet, Dornan's Late Late Show appearances are not solely focused on the dramatic. He is known for his infectious sense of humor and willingness to participate in lighthearted sketches and games. One memorable instance involved him and Tubridy attempting to master the intricacies of hurling, Ireland's national sport. The skit showcased Dornan's athleticism and playful spirit, reminding viewers that he's more than just a brooding heartthrob.

Dornan's musical talents have also been on display during his Late Late Show visits. He has performed impromptu acoustic renditions of popular songs, showcasing his vocal abilities and musicality. These performances add another dimension to his persona, revealing a well-rounded artist with a passion for music beyond acting.

Of course, no discussion of Dornan's Late Late Show appearances is complete without mentioning his association with the "Fifty Shades" franchise. While he acknowledges the film's cultural impact, he is refreshingly candid about his perspective on them. He readily engages in good-natured jokes and anecdotes about the films, demonstrating his ability to laugh at himself and avoid taking them too seriously.

In conclusion, Jamie Dornan's appearances on The Late Late Show have been a captivating blend of personal stories, humor, and artistic expression. He has connected with audiences on a deep level, showcasing his vulnerability, charm, and talent. His visits are a testament to his multifaceted personality and his ability to captivate viewers with his genuine Irish spirit.

Here are some additional facts and trivia about Jamie Dornan's Late Late Show appearances:

- His first appearance was in 2013, shortly after the release of "Fifty Shades of Grey."
- He has appeared on the show alongside other notable guests, including Saoirse Ronan, Michael Fassbender, and Liam Neeson.
- He has won over the hearts of many Irish viewers, solidifying his status as a national treasure.
- His appearances are often trending on social media, highlighting his enduring popularity.

Whether discussing his latest project, sharing personal stories, or simply laughing with Ryan Tubridy, Jamie

Dornan's visits to The Late Late Show are always a highlight. He continues to leave viewers wanting more, eager for his next appearance on the iconic Irish talk show.

CONCLUSION

As we reach the culmination of our exploration into the life and soul of Jamie Dornan, we find ourselves not at the end of a neatly woven narrative, but rather at the vibrant tapestry of his ongoing journey. The man we have encountered is far more than just the sum of his roles, headlines, or chiseled features. He is a multifaceted individual, an artist constantly evolving, a family man cherishing his loved ones, and a compassionate soul extending his reach beyond the spotlight.

Dornan's artistic pursuit thrives on a relentless exploration of diverse avenues. From the brooding intensity of Christian Grey to the heartwarming vulnerability of Pa in "Belfast," he fearlessly embraces challenges and defies typecasting. His upcoming projects, ranging from the adrenaline-fueled "Heart of Stone" to the chilling "A Haunting in Venice," hint at the breadth of his artistic repertoire and his unwavering commitment to pushing boundaries.

Beyond the screen, Dornan's life revolves around the unwavering love and support he shares with his wife and daughters. Fatherhood has become a guiding principle, influencing his career choices and prioritizing roles that allow him to be present for his family. The recent health scare in Portugal served as a poignant reminder of life's fragility, yet Dornan's resilience and the love surrounding him propelled him towards a full recovery. He emerged with a renewed appreciation for the preciousness of time and the importance of cherishing loved ones. Dornan's compassion extends far beyond his immediate circle. His dedication to various charitable causes reflects a genuine desire to contribute to a better world. He lends his voice to environmental issues, advocates for children's health, and actively participates in fundraising events. His platform isn't just a source of fame; it's a tool for positive change, a testament to his inherent kindness and unwavering desire to make a difference.

The Jamie Dornan we have unveiled is not simply a Hollywood heartthrob or a brooding billionaire. He is a tapestry woven with threads of artistic ambition, unwavering family devotion, and genuine compassion. He is a man who embraces challenges, cherishes his loved ones, and uses his platform to make the world a better place. As he continues to navigate the complexities of life, career, and fatherhood, his journey remains captivating, promising new artistic endeavors, heartwarming moments with his family, and continued contributions to causes close to his heart.

This book is not an ending, but rather an invitation to keep following the ever-evolving tapestry of Jamie Dornan. With his talent, dedication, and genuine humanity, he is sure to continue surprising, inspiring, and captivating audiences for years to come. So, turn the final page, not with a sense of closure, but with an anticipation for the next chapter in the enthralling story of Jamie Dornan, the man who proves that beneath the shades lies a tapestry woven with artistry, heart, and genuine humanity.

Printed in Great Britain
by Amazon

c8e20e85-a97a-45d8-8d54-45044129f6bdR01